Scaleville: Building a World of Number
Grades 3-4
by Jeannie Ruiz

Scaleville: Building a World of Number (Revised 2023 Grade 5-6 Edition

Copyright 2023 by Jeannie Ruiz

Published by Printing Futures, Vancouver WA

ISBN 978-1-942357-73-5

Photo permissions and authors, illustrators, designers, photographers available for download at the URL.

http://www.PrintingFutures.com

The Reasoning Behind "Reasonableness"
Scale and Estimation

Teacher: Do you think this answer is "reasonable"? Your calculation says that loading 2 adult male elephants onto a plane will add 682.7 pounds.

Student: Oh, that doesn't make sense does it? If two elephants weigh about 700 pounds then each would only be around 350 pounds. An NFL lineman or sumo wrestler weighs about 300 pounds and an adult elephant weighs a lot more than those. Maybe I have the decimal in the wrong place

Ten80 viewpoint

Every student should be able to engage in a discussion like this.

Recognizing an unreasonable answer is difficult unless one knows how much things weigh, how fast they move, how much area they cover. Students only need a few mental landmarks to enable them to estimate to the nearest power of ten. Will the answer be closer to 20, 200, 2,000 or 20,000? As estimation skills improve, reasonableness becomes a meaningful concept.

Scaleville is a set of daily class starters. Used regularly, students will gain a sense of number. You will build fundamental skills in estimation, an understanding of measure and a physical connection to scale. How much does a racing bike weigh? How fast does it go? How fast does a baby crawl? How tall is a giraffe? How tall are you? How much, how far, how fast, how much...

Scaleville Daily Starters

Welcome to SCALEVILLE, *a world of numbers*. In this set of Scaleville Daily Starters, you will be asked to describe many ordinary and some not-so-ordinary things in several quantitative ways. These 180 activities are a great way to kick-off any math or science session.

- A reference table is included in the back of this book, but use it only to check your completed work.
- Project the SCALEVILLE DAILY activities, view them on a computer screen or print them in black-and-white using the electronic files provided.
- Print or view the electronic file called SCALEVILLE DAILY NOTES for information on each activity. Many activity notes include connections between the numbers, science and/or history.
- Use the five-day answer sheet to complete a full week of activities on one page.
- The first Scaleville lesson may take as long as 20 or 30 minutes. The allotted time will decrease to roughly five minutes as you or your students become more comfortable with measurement, unit conversion, powers of ten and estimation.
- Though you or your students are encouraged to complete all steps, unit conversions (step #3) and/or powers of ten (step #4) may not be required or appropriate for everyone. Developing an intuitive understanding of the numbers is far more beneficial to long-term success in problem-solving.
- On this Earth, weight and mass are approximately equal; however, weight and mass are very different properties. Where mass is required in these activities, the proper units of kilograms (kg) or multiples of kilograms should be used.

Learn to speak math, the language of science!

NCTM Standards

Grades 3-4 Expectations: In grades 3-4 all students should–

- understand various meanings of multiplication and division;
- understand the effects of multiplying and dividing whole numbers;
- develop and use strategies to estimate the results of whole-number computations and to judge the reasonableness of such results;
- develop and use strategies to estimate computations involving fractions and decimals in situations relevant to students' experience.

Grades 5-8 Expectations: In grades5-8 all students should–

- compare and order fractions, decimals, and percents efficiently and find their approximate locations on a number line;
- develop meaning for percents greater than 100 and less than 1;
- understand and use ratios and proportions to represent quantitative relationships;
- develop an understanding of large numbers and recognize and appropriately use exponential, scientific, and calculator notation;
- develop meaning for integers and represent and compare quantities with them develop and use strategies to estimate the results of rational-number computations and judge the reasonableness of the results.

Example Activity & Answers

Write in this book or repeat activities many times by using the Scaleville Daily worksheet available on the Scaleville Daily CD-ROM.

Distance and Speed

Step # 1

How fast does a bumble bee fly?
About 14 miles per hour

Hint: Can you outrun a bee?

Step # 2

Name something 10 times as fast.
High hurricane winds or the top speed of a car

Name something 1/10th as fast.

A turtle swimming very fast

Step # 3

Convert the measurement from # 1 to metric.
Convert to standard if already in metric.

$$\frac{14\ miles}{1\ hour} \times \frac{5280\ feet}{1\ mile} \times \frac{1\ meter}{3.28\ feet} = 22{,}531\ meters\ per\ hour$$

Step # 4

The measurement from #1 falls between what two powers of ten?

$$10^{1} \quad and \quad 10^{2}$$

Table of Contents

Some Symbol Definitions

Length / Distance
inch = in
yard = yd
feet = ft
meter = m
micrometer = micron
yard = yd

Mass and Weight
pound = lb
gram = g

Speed
miles per hour = mph
kilometers per hour = kph
inches per second = in / sec
feet per second = ft / sec
meters per second = m / sec
centimeters per second = cm / sec

Volume
fluid ounces = fl. oz.
gallons = gal

Power and Energy
watts = W
joules = J
British Thermal Units = BTU
nutritional calorie = Cal

Pressure
pounds per square feet = lb/ft^2
pounds per square inch = psi
Pascal = Pa

Powers and Multipliers
squared (symbol) = $(symbol)^2$
cubed (symbol) = $(symbol)^3$
nano = 10^{-9} = n
mili = 10^{-3} = m
centi = 10^{-2} = c
kilo = $x\ 10^3$ = k
Mega = $x\ 10^6$ = M
Giga = $x\ 10^9$ = G
Tera = $x\ 10^{12}$ = T

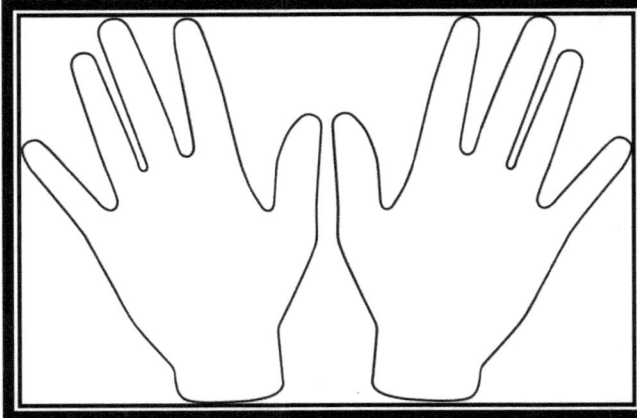

DRAW OR COLOR

The first section has suggested images.
Use your imagination to help you remember
the scale of how thing move and look.

Distance and Speed

Activity 1

What object, building or monument is 1 mile from your school?

Hint: 1 mile takes about 15 minutes to walk or just a minute to drive on the highway.

Write your answer here.

Draw / Color

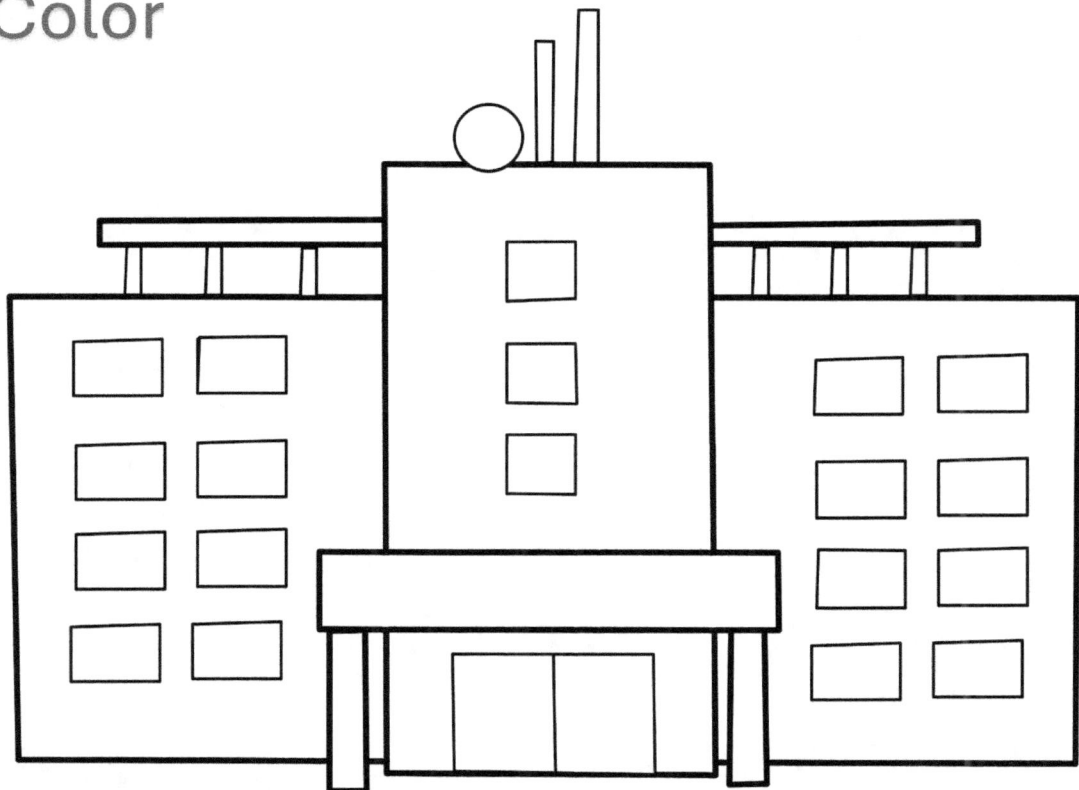

Distance and Speed
Activity 2

Step # 1
How long is a grown mama giraffe's body?

The giraffe's neck is 1/3rd the length of its entire body. How long is a giraffe's neck?

Write your answer here.

Draw and Color the Giraffe's at Home

Distance and Speed

Activity 3

What is your height in standard units of measure?

Standard units are those we use most often in America.

Write your answer here.

Draw / Color

Distance and Speed

Activity 4

Step # 1

How tall is your desk?

Is it adjustable? What is its maximum height?

Write your answer here.

Draw / Color

Distance and Speed

Activity 5

How long is a flea?

Fleas have been known to jump nearly 200 times their body length.

What distance is that jump?

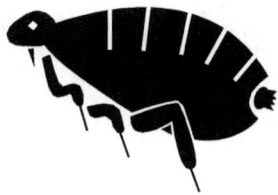

Write your answer here.

Draw / Color

Where might a flea live?

dog

puppy

Distance and Speed

Activity 6

Step # 1

What are the length & width of a paperback book cover?

What will you be able to calculate if you know a rectangular object's length & width?

Write your answer here.

Draw / Color

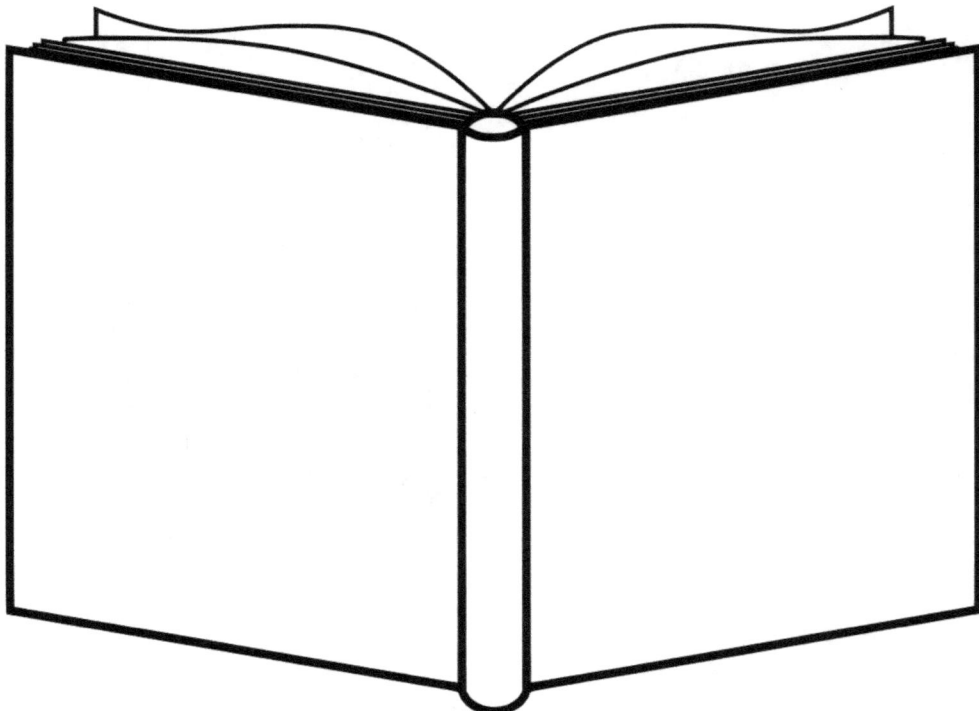

Distance and Speed

Activity 7

The smallest bird in the world is about the same length as a grasshopper. How long is the world's smallest bird?

Write your answer here.

Draw / Color

Distance and Speed

Activity 8

Step # 1

Geckos can stick to almost any surface, including ceilings. They can do this because they have more than 1 billion tiny hairs on their toes. What is the diameter of each of these hairs?

Hint: They are about 1/500th the diameter of a human hair.

Write your answer here.

Draw / Color

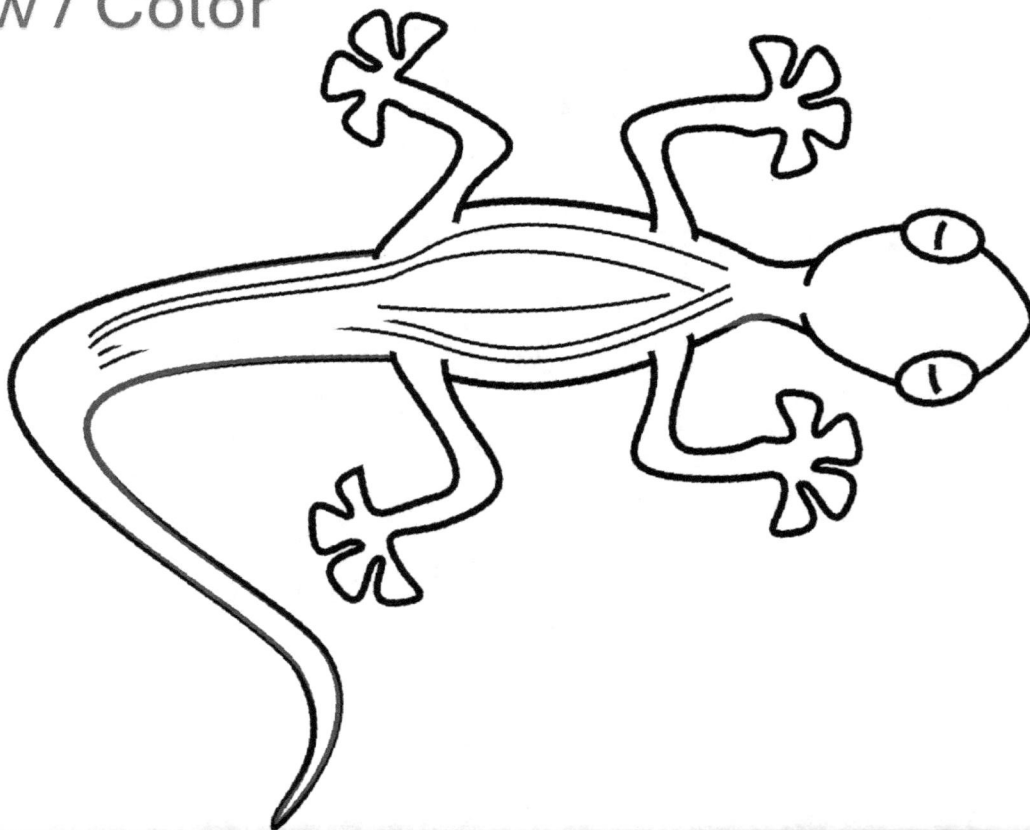

Distance and Speed

Activity 11

How long is your hand?

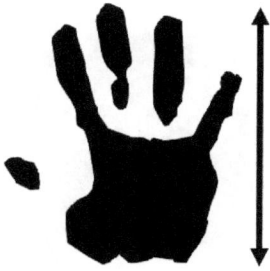

Measure from fingertip to wrist.

Write your answer here.

Draw / Color

Distance and Speed

Activity 12

Step # 1

What is the diameter of a nickel?

The diameter is a straight line from edge to edge, passing through the center of the circle.

By the way, Thomas Jefferson has been on the U.S. nickel since 1938.

Write your answer here.

Draw / Color

Distance and Speed

Activity 13

What is the diameter of a CD?

The average CD measures 14.69 inches around its outer edge.

Write your answer here.

Draw / Color

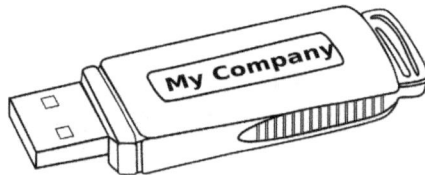 

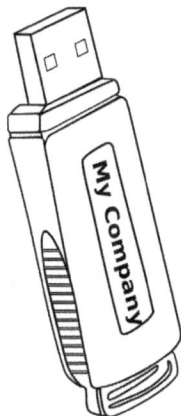 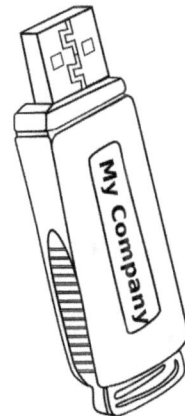

Distance and Speed

Activity 14

Step # 1

What is the distance around your neck? Measure just below the Adam's apple.

Your Adam's apple is the bump in your neck that is actually your voice box or larynx.

Write your answer here.

Draw / Color

Distance and Speed

Activity 15

What is your arm span, the length from fingertip to fingertip?

What is your height? Do you notice any correlation (match) between the two measures?

Write your answer here.

Draw / Color

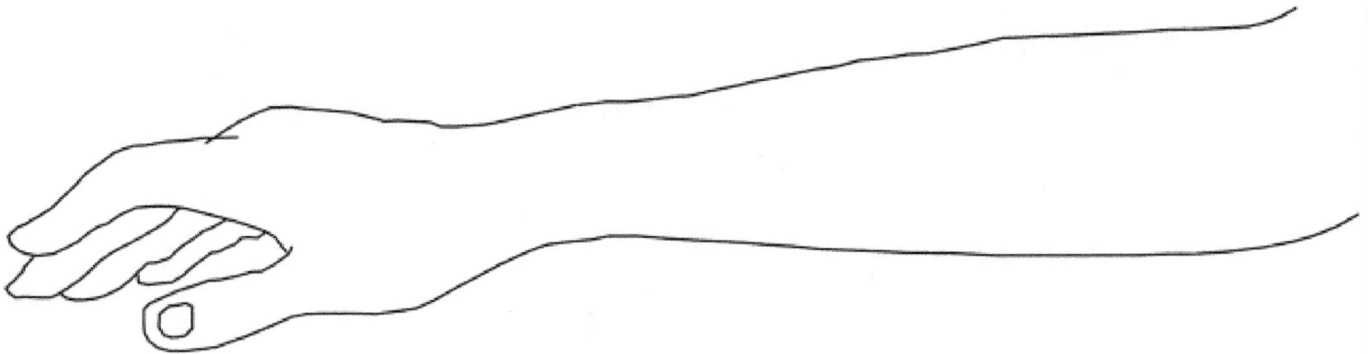

Distance and Speed
Activity 16

Step # 1

What is the average wingspan of an American eagle?

An Eagle's wingspan is wider than an average man is tall.

Write your answer here.

Draw / Color

Distance and Speed

How long is your classroom whiteboard or chalkboard?

Measure the length.

Write your answer here.

Draw / Color

Distance and Speed

Activity 18

Step # 1

The giraffe is about 3 times taller than the average man. How tall is a giraffe?

Think about the height of an average man then estimate the giraffe's height.

Write your answer here.

Draw / Color

Distance and Speed

What is the average height of a willow oak tree?

How many times taller than you is that?

Write your answer here.

Draw / Color

Enlarge pattern 200%

Distance and Speed

Activity 24

Step # 1

How tall is the Statue of Liberty when measured from her feet to the torch?

The tallest living redwood on record stands 367 feet. It is 62 feet taller than the Statue of Liberty as measured from the very base to the torch.

Write your answer here.

Draw / Color

Distance and Speed

Activity 25

How long is each outer wall of the
Pentagon building?

What is the total length of outer walls?
Use your estimate for each wall then use
the number of sides on a Pentagon to
estimate the total length.

Write your answer here.

Draw / Color

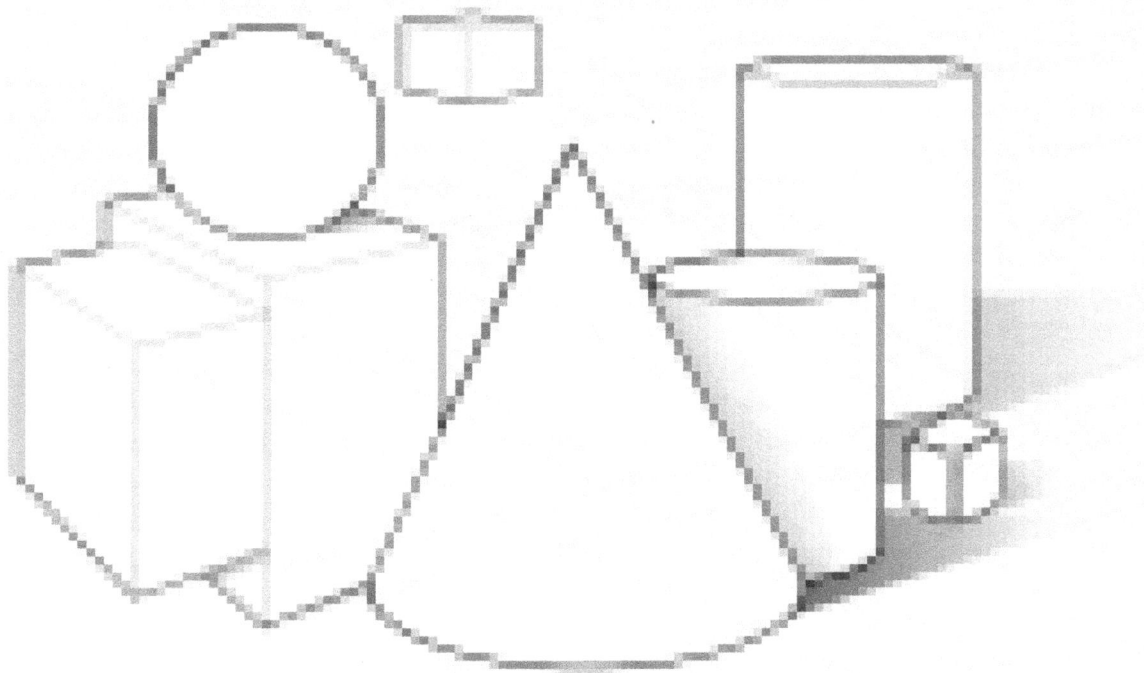

Distance and Speed

Activity 26

Step # 1

What is the height of the Eiffel Tower in Paris, France?

Write your answer here.

Draw / Color

Distance and Speed

What object is about a mile and a half from your school?

Write your answer here.

Draw / Color

Distance and Speed

Step # 1

What is the height of Mt. Everest, the tallest mountain in the world?

What is the second tallest mountain?

What country is it in?

Write your answer here.

Draw / Color

Distance and Speed

What is the legal speed on a rural U.S. Interstate Highway?

How fast does your family drive on the highway?

Write your answer here.

Draw / Color

Distance and Speed

Step # 1

How fast can you run?

Use several stopwatches to get a more accurate time. Average the times over several trials.

Write your answer here.

Draw / Color

Distance and Speed

Activity 40

How fast does a spider travel?
In other words, how far can a spider move in 1 minute?

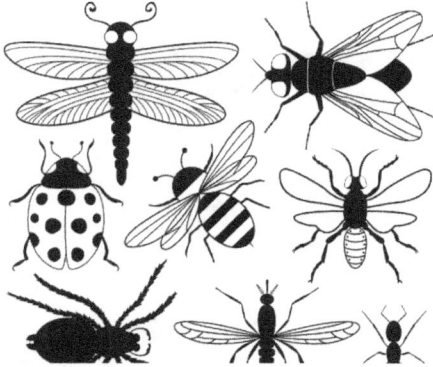

Some spiders could beat a tortoise in a foot race!

Write your answer here.

Color the Picture.

Distance and Speed

Activity 41

Step # 1

What is the record-breaking speed of a garden snail?

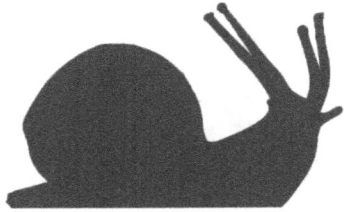

It was set by a mollusk named Archie.

How far do you think Archie could move in 1 minute?

Write your answer here.

Draw / Color

Distance and Speed

Activity 45

How fast does a giant tortoise move?

It is slightly faster than the three-toed sloth, the slowest mammal in the world.

Write your answer here.

Draw / Color

Distance and Speed
Activity 46

Step # 1
What is the speed of a baby crawling?

Babies crawl faster than turtles.

Write your answer here.

Draw / Color

Distance and Speed

What is the speed of a fast walker?

How fast can you walk?

Write your answer here.

Draw / Color

Distance and Speed

Activity 48

Step # 1

How fast does a bumble bee fly?

Could you outrun a bee?

Write your answer here.

Draw / Color

Distance and Speed

Activity 49

What is the speed of a butterfly?

Do you move faster than a butterfly?

Write your answer here.

Draw / Color

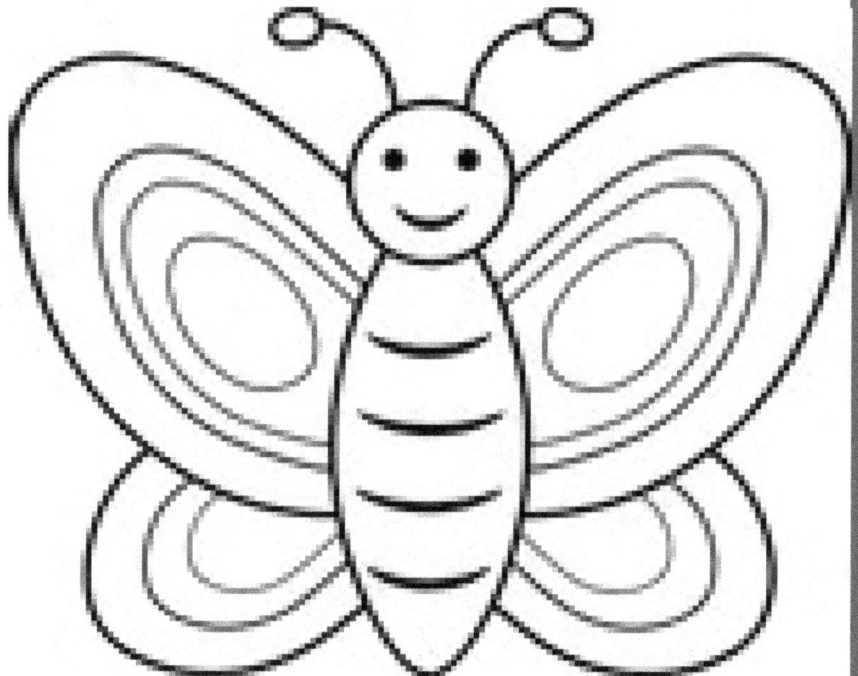

Distance and Speed

Activity 50

Step # 1

What is a top speed of a human sprinter over 220 yards?

There are 3 feet in every yard, so 220 yds is 660 feet.

How fast can you sprint 220 yards?

Write your answer here.

Draw / Color

Distance and Speed
Activity 51

What is the speed of a roller blade speed skater?

Is this faster or slower than a professional cyclist?

Write your answer here.

Draw / Color

Distance and Speed

Activity 53

Step # 1

Remember our 14 to 18 feet-tall giraffe?
What is its top running speed?

Write your answer here.

Draw / Color

Distance and Speed

What is the speed of a racing bicycle?

How fast can you ride?
How does your bicycle differ from a professional cycle?

Write your answer here.

Draw / Color

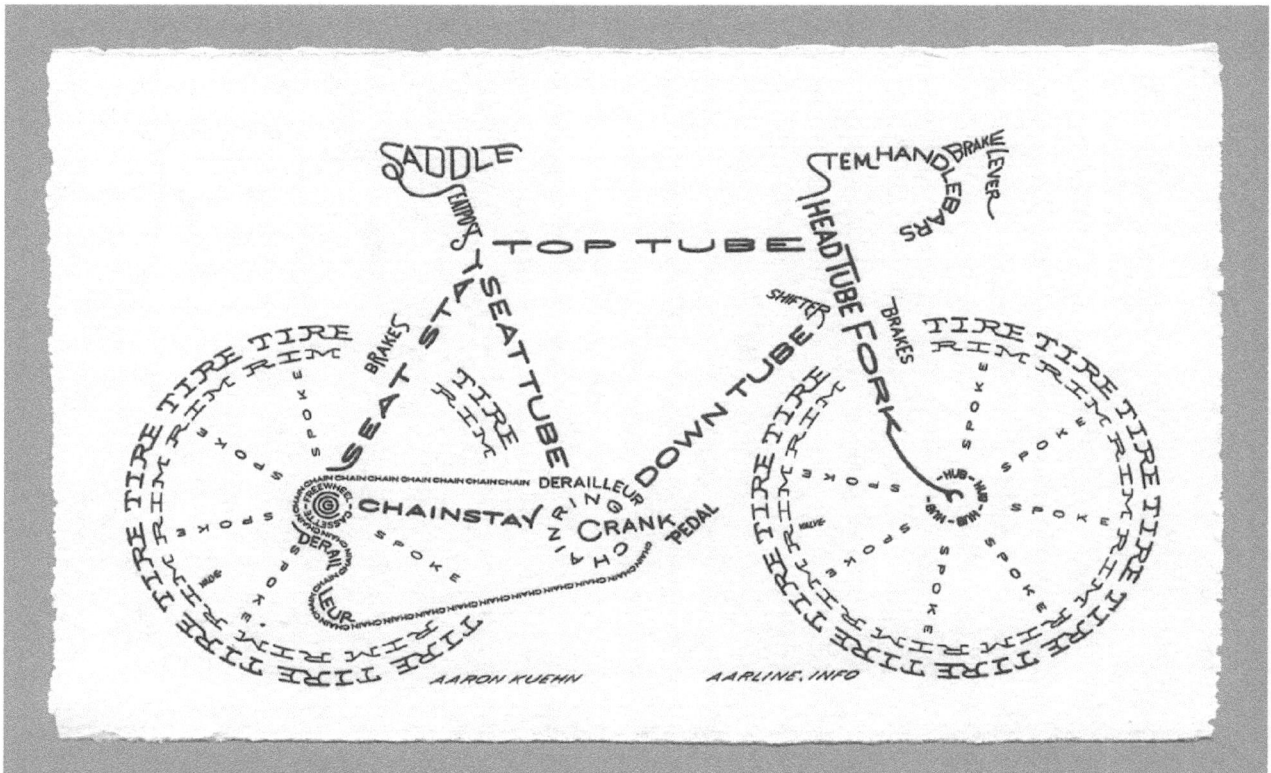

SADDLE STEM HANDLE BARS BRAKE LEVER
TOP TUBE HEAD TUBE
SEAT STAY SEAT TUBE DOWN TUBE FORK SHIFTER BRAKES
TIRE TIRE RIM BRAKES RIM TIRE TIRE RIM
SPOKE DERAILLEUR SPOKE
CHAINSTAY RING CRANK PEDAL HUB VALVE
DERAILLEUR CHAIN SPOKE
FREEWHEEL CASSETTE

AARON KUEHN   AARLINE.INFO

Distance and Speed

Activity 57

Step # 1

According to the San Diego Natural History Museum, "a frightened house cat can run up to 30 miles per hour."

A cheetah runs more than twice as fast. How fast does a cheetah run?

Write your answer here.

Draw / Color

Distance and Speed

What is the top speed record of a standard-production American car?

Would a standard heavy truck travel faster or slower?

Write your answer here.

Draw / Color

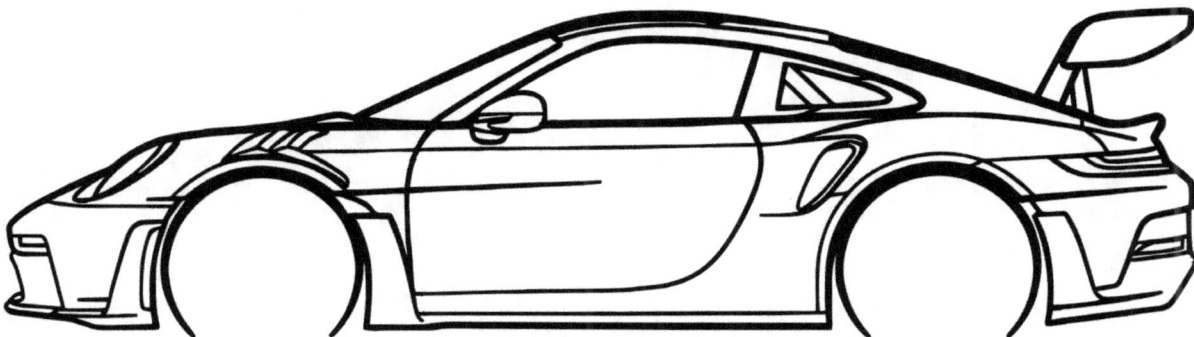

Mass and Weight
Activity 76

Step # 1

What is the weight of a golf ball?

Is that heavier than a mouse?

Write your answer here.

Draw / Color

Did you know a golf ball has about 300–500 tiny dimples — and those dimples actually help it fly farther and straighter through the air?

Mass and Weight

What is the weight of a baby rabbit?

What is the weight of an average human baby?

Write your answer here.

Draw / Color

Rabbit

🐰 *Did you know a rabbit's ears can be over 4 inches long — and they help it stay cool as well as hear danger from far away?*

Mass and Weight

Step # 1

What is the weight of a kitten?

Is that heavier than a rabbit?

Write your answer here.

Draw / Color

Cat

🐱 *Did you know most cats can jump up to six times their body length in one leap — that's like a person jumping over a school bus!*

Mass and Weight

What is the weight of a pair of roller blade skates, plus helmet and pads?

How many of your math books equal the weight of these items?

Write your answer here.

Draw / Color

Skates

Did you know the first ice skates were made from animal bones over 4,000 years ago — and people slid across frozen lakes on them?

Mass and Weight

Activity 80

Step # 1

What is the weight of a racing bicycle?

How does that compare to the weight of a dirt bike?

Write your answer here.

Draw / Color

Bikes

🚲 *Did you know the fastest cyclists can reach speeds over 60 miles per hour — about as fast as a car on an interstate highway!*

Mass and Weight

Activity 81

What is the weight of a big dog?

What is the average weight of your classmate's dogs? Cats? Goldfish?

Write your answer here.

Draw / Color

Goldfish

Did you know goldfish never stop growing — they just grow slower in small tanks, but in a big pond they can reach over a foot long!

Mass and Weight

Activity 82

Step # 1

What is the average weight of a male adult?

What is the average weight of a female adult?

Write your answer here.

Draw / Color

Human (Male vs. Female)

Did you know that on average, adult males weigh about 30 pounds more than adult females — but everyone's healthy weight depends on height and build?

Mass and Weight
Activity 83

What is the weight of a large adult male dolphin?

How does that compare to the weight of a female dolphin?

Write your answer here.

Draw / Color

Dolphin

Did you know dolphins can swim up to 20 miles per hour — about as fast as a car driving through a neighborhood?

Mass and Weight

Step # 1

What is the weight of a typical adult male alligator?

Is this similar to a big or a small sea lion?

Write your answer here.

Draw / Color

Alligator

🐊 *Did you know alligators can grow more than a foot every year when they're young — and some reach over 13 feet long as adults?*

Mass and Weight

What is the weight of a baby grand piano?

What would cause the piano to weigh more on a rainy day?

Write your answer here.

Draw / Color

Piano

🎹 *Did you know a full-size piano has 88 keys and can weigh as much as 1,000 pounds — that's heavier than a baby grand SUV tire!*

Mass and Weight

Activity 87

Step # 1

What is the weight of a typical racehorse?

Is that heavier than a walrus?

Write your answer here.

Draw / Color

Horse

🐎 *Did you know an average horse weighs roughly the same as a small car?*

Mass and Weight

Activity 88

What is the weight of small car?

Is that heavier than a small plane?

Write your answer here.

Draw / Color

Racecar

Did you know a professional racecar can weigh less than a regular car — around 3,000 pounds — but it can still go more than 200 miles per hour?

Mass and Weight

Activity 89

Step # 1

What is the weight of a large male African Elephant?

What about a large female African elephant?

Write your answer here.

Draw / Color

Elephant

🐘 *Did you know an adult African elephant can weigh about the same as six small cars!*

Mass and Weight

Activity 101

What is the mass of the Earth's Oceans (in kg)?

What portion of the Earth's mass is found in the oceans?

Write your answer here.

Draw / Color

Earth's Oceans

Did you know Earth's oceans weigh more than **1.4 quintillion tons** — that's a 1 followed by 18 zeros! They cover about 70% of our planet.

Mass and Weight
Activity 102

Step # 1

What is the mass of Earth?

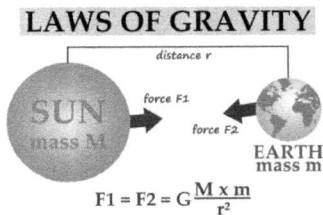

LAWS OF GRAVITY

distance r

SUN
mass M

force F1

force F2

EARTH
mass m

$$F1 = F2 = G\frac{M \times m}{r^2}$$

How does that compare to the planet Mercury?

Write your answer here.

Draw / Color

Earth

🌍 *Did you know planet Earth weighs about* **13,170,000,000,000,000,000,000,000 pounds** — *that's 13 septillion! Luckily, gravity holds it all together.*

Mass and Weight

What is the mass of the planet Jupiter?

How many times more massive is Jupiter than the Earth?

Write your answer here.

Draw / Color

Jupiter

🪐 *Did you know Jupiter is more than* **300 times heavier than Earth** *— it's so massive that it could fit over 1,300 Earths inside it!*

Mass and Weight
Activity 104

Step # 1
What is the mass of the Sun?

How does that compare to the most massive white dwarf star?

Write your answer here.

Draw / Color

Horse
🐎 *Did you know an average horse weighs about 1,000 pounds — roughly the same as a small car?*

Area and Volume

Step # 1

What is the area of a computer pixel?

Computer monitors typically display between 72 and 100 pixels per inch (ppi).

Write your answer here.

Draw / Color

Airline Food Trays

🍱 *Did you know every food tray on an airplane has to fit perfectly like a puzzle piece — so airlines design them to match the exact space of your seat's tray table?*

Area and Volume

What is the area of the top of a flat-head pin?

Give your answer in square inches (in²).

Write your answer here.

Draw / Color

Flathead Pins

🍷 *Did you know sewing pins are measured in "millimeters," and the flathead pin is often **38 mm long** — about the width of two crayons end to end?*

Area and Volume

Step # 1

What is the area of a standard postage stamp?

Some special stamps are bigger. What might that area be?

How much does a stamp cost now?

Write your answer here.

Draw / Color

Postage Stamps

*Did you know the first U.S. postage stamp cost just **5 cents** in 1847 — and today, a single stamp can carry a letter thousands of miles?*

Area and Volume
Activity 109

What is the area of an average airline food tray?

Is it similar to your cafeteria tray?

Write your answer here.

Draw / Color

📍 **Fun Fact for Students**

Did you know flathead pins were invented to help fabrics stay smooth while sewing? Their flat tops let you sew right over them — no bumps allowed!

Pins have been used for thousands of years and were first made from bone or bronze.

Area and Volume

Step # 1

The amount of energy that clouds remove from a 6 ft² patch of land is equal to the energy from a 60 watt light bulb. What are some possible measurements (length and width) of that land if it is rectangular?

length x width = area
There are many answers.

Write your answer here.

Draw / Color

Light Bulbs

💡 *Did you know the inside of a light bulb isn't empty — it's filled with gas that helps the filament glow without burning up?!*

Area and Volume

What is the area of skin covering an average adult man?

In other words, what is his surface area?

Write your answer here.

Draw / Color

Human Skin

✋ *Did you know your skin is your body's largest organ — and if you could stretch it out, it would cover about **20 square feet**, the size of a small blanket?*

Area and Volume

Step # 1

What are the dimensions of a ping pong table? In other words, what is the length (L) and width (W)?

What is the area of a ping pong table? L x W = Area

Write your answer here.

Draw / Color

Ping Pong

*Did you know a ping pong ball weighs only **2.7 grams** — lighter than a single sheet of paper!*

Area and Volume

What is the average area of a parking space for a car?

How much bigger would it be for a bus?

Write your answer here.

Draw / Color

Buses

🚌 *Did you know a full-size school bus can weigh more than **25,000 pounds** — about as much as five elephants?!*

Area and Volume

Step # 1

What is the ceiling area of your classroom?

How does this compare to the floor area of your classroom?

Write your answer here.

Draw / Color

Classrooms

🏫 *Did you know an average classroom clock ticks about **43,200 times a day** — that's one tick for every second students are learning!*

Area and Volume

What is the length and width of an American football field?

What are the areas of other sports fields?

Write your answer here.

Draw / Color

Football Field
Did you know a football field, including the end zones, is about **1.3 acres** of playing space!

Area and Volume

Step # 1

What is the base area of the Great
Pyramid of Giza?

Remember that the height is 480 feet.

Write your answer here.

Draw / Color

Pyramid

▲ *Did you know the Great Pyramid
of Giza covers about **13 acres** at its
base — that's like **9 football fields** of
stone!*

Area and Volume

What is the land area covered by the
Pentagon building?

How much of that is the inner courtyard
(center of the Pentagon)?

Write your answer here.

Draw / Color

The Pentagon

🏢 *Did you know The Pentagon building
has **6.5 million square feet** of floor
space — and enough hallways to walk
17 miles without going outside?*

Area and Volume

Step # 1

What is the land area covered by parking spaces for the Pentagon building?

How many spaces is that?

> Write your answer here.

Draw / Color

Basement

🏠 *Did you know the world's deepest basement is in a gold mine in South Africa — more than **2 miles** below the ground?*

Area and Volume

What is the floor area within the Pentagon building?

There are 5 floors including the basement and mezzanine.

Write your answer here.

Draw / Color

Floor
🪵 *Did you know the world's largest floor is in an airplane factory — big enough to hold **75 football fields** inside?*

Mezzanine
🎭 *Did you know a mezzanine is a "half floor" often found in theaters — it lets more people fit without making the building taller!*

Area and Volume
Activity 120

Step # 1

According to the U.S. Census, what is the land area of the Borough of Manhattan in New York?

Write your answer here.

Draw / Color

Did you know that Manhattan (New York County) is the most densely populated county in the United States? It is among the smallest in land area.

Area and Volume

What is the land area of the island of Bali, Indonesia?

Write your answer here.

Draw / Color

Indonesia

🌋 *Did you know Indonesia is made up of **over 17,000 islands** — together they cover an area almost as wide as the United States!*

Area and Volume

Step # 1

What is the published land area of the state of Texas?

What state has more land area than Texas? Does that state have a higher or lower population density than Texas?

Write your answer here.

Draw / Color

Texas

🐵 *Did you know Texas is so big that you could fit **France, Belgium, and the Netherlands** inside it — and still have room left over!*

Area and Volume

What is the published land area of the United States?

How long is each side of the smallest square in which the US would fit?

Write your answer here.

Draw / Color

Maps

Did you know no map can show Earth's true size perfectly — flat maps stretch some places to make the round planet fit on paper!

Area and Volume

Step # 1

What is the published surface area of the Earth?

How much of that is under water?

Write your answer here.

Draw / Color

Water on Earth

Did you know about **70% of Earth's surface** is covered by water — but only **3%** of it is fresh water we can drink?

Area and Volume

What is the surface area of the planet Neptune?

NEPTUNE

Write your answer here.

Draw / Color

Neptune

🔵 *Did you know Neptune could hold* **57 Earths** *inside it — it's the farthest planet from the Sun and made mostly of swirling gas and ice!*

Area and Volume

Step # 1

What is the volume of a small sugar cube?

How many cubes make up a cup of sugar?

Write your answer here.

Draw / Color

Sugar

🍬 *Did you know one teaspoon of sugar has about **4 grams** — and that's the same weight as a small paperclip?*

Area and Volume

Activity 127

What is the volume of a milk carton from the school cafeteria?

Read the carton!

Write your answer here.

Draw / Color

Milk

*Did you know it takes about **10 pounds of milk** to make just **1 pound of cheese**?*

Area and Volume

Step # 1

What is the volume of a two-serving plastic soda bottle?

How much more soda is held by a family size bottle? Which bottle is the better financial bargain?

Write your answer here.

Draw / Color

Plastic Bottles

♻ *Did you know Americans use about **50 billion plastic bottles** every year — and recycling just one saves enough energy to power a light bulb for 3 hours!*

Area and Volume

Activity 129

What is the volume of a tissue box?

The volume of a rectangle can be calculated by multiplying the height, length and width. Estimate the three dimensions.

Volume = length × width × height

Write your answer here.

Draw / Color

Tissue Paper

Did you know tissue paper is so light that **100 sheets** weigh less than **a single apple**?

Area and Volume
Activity 130

Step # 1

What is the average capacity of a party balloon?

Capacity is a measure of how much space an object occupies.

Write your answer here.

Draw / Color

Balloons

🎈 *Did you know a balloon expands about **ten times its size** when filled with air — that's why it feels stretchy when you blow it up!*

Area and Volume

What is the volume of a large cereal box?

Estimate the three dimensions.
Volume = length × width × depth
OR, since Area = length × width
Volume = area x depth

Write your answer here.

Draw / Color

Cereal Box

🥣 *Did you know if you flatten a cereal box, you can measure its area — it's just one big rectangle made from thin cardboard!*

Area and Volume

Step # 1

What is the radius of the top of a soda can?

The radius is any line segment with one endpoint on the circle and the other at the center of the circle.

Write your answer here.

Draw / Color

Soda Can

🥤 *Did you know a soda can holds* **12 ounces**, *or about* **355 milliliters** — *roughly the same volume as a small measuring cup?*

Area and Volume

What is the radius of the bottom of a medium pie tin?

The radius is any line segment with one endpoint on the circle and the other at the center of the circle.

Write your answer here.

Draw / Color

Did you know "tin foil" isn't really tin anymore? It used to be made from real tin, but now it's aluminum — shiny, light, and perfect for wrapping leftovers!

Aluminum is lighter, cheaper and doesn't make your food taste funny like real tin did.

Area and Volume

...and components of volume

Activity 134

Step # 1

What is the diameter of the bottom of a medium pie tin?

Pie tins are labeled by their diameter. The diameter of a circle is any straight line that passes through the center and whose endpoints are on the circular boundary

Write your answer here.

Draw / Color

Did you know **pi (3.14)** helps you find the area of your pie tin? Without pi, we'd never know how much pie fits inside!

Area and Volume
...and components of volume
Activity 135

What is the circumference of the bottom of a typical apple pie?

Circumference is the distance around a closed curve (circle). You can use a string to measure the tin's circumference.

Write your answer here.

Draw / Color

*Did you know math teachers love pie day — because March 14th is **3/14**, the same as **pi (3.14)**!*

Area and Volume
...and components of volume
Activity 136

Step # 1

What is the circumference of a tortilla that has a radius of 6 inches?

Circumference = Pi x (2 x radius).
What other measurement is equal to (2 x radius)?

Facts about Pi
Pi is estimated as 3.14
Pi has no units
Pi is represented by the symbol called Pi, Π

Write your answer here.

Draw / Color

Rolling Pin
*Did you know a typical rolling pin is about **18 inches long** — that's the same as a ruler and a half!*

Area and Volume
...and components of volume
Activity 137

Step # 1
What is the bottom area of a medium pie tin?

Area of a circle is equal to:
Pi x radius x radius = Pi x radius^2
Or, estimated as:
$\qquad$ 3.14 x radius^2

Write your answer here.

Draw / Color

Did you know every pie has a secret ingredient — **pi (3.14)**! It's the number we use to measure how big a circle is! — so the next time you eat pie, you're really doing math!

Area and Volume

Step # 1

What is the approximate volume of a medium pie tin? Estimate by assuming that the wall is vertical (straight up and down).

Estimate the tin's volume as a cylinder using this formula:

(Area of pi tin base) x tin depth, or

(Pi x radius²) x tin depth

Write your answer here.

Draw / Color

Pie Tin

🔘 *Did you know most pie tins are **9 inches wide** — and that's why we call a round dessert a "9-inch pie"?*

Area and Volume
Activity 139

What are the dimensions of a standard large suitcase?

First estimate the dimensions of the suitcase. What is its length, width and height?

Write your answer here.

Draw / Color

Suitcase

🧳 *Did you know the world's largest suitcase was over **10 feet tall** — big enough to fit a whole family inside (but no airline would check it in!)*

Area and Volume

Step # 1

What is the volume of a standard barrel of oil?

Have you heard 'barrels of oil' mentioned in the news lately?

Write your answer here.

Draw / Color

Oil Barrel

🛢 *Did you know one oil barrel holds **42 gallons** — about the same as **84 two-liter soda bottles**?*

Area and Volume

What is the capacity of a standard 3-4 person hot air balloon?

How much time do you think is required to fill that balloon?
Minutes? Hours? Days?

Write your answer here.

Draw / Color

Hot Air Balloon
🎈 *Did you know a hot air balloon is so big it can hold enough air to lift a small car!*

Area and Volume

Activity 142

Step # 1

What is the typical volume of an Olympic swimming pool?

What measurements do you need to find a solution? What assumption could you make to calculate the volume?

Write your answer here.

Draw / Color

Olympic Swimming Pool

*Did you know an Olympic swimming pool holds about the same water as **10,000 bathtubs**?*

Area and Volume

How much water is in a typical water tower?

How many Olympic swimming pools does this hold?

Write your answer here.

Draw / Color

Water Towers

🚰 Did you know water towers work by gravity — a single tower can hold **a million gallons** of water and push it through pipes to your sink? water!

Area and Volume

Step # 1

Approximately how many gallons of water are in the Loch Ness lake in Scotland?

If Nessy the fictional Lock Ness monster left the lake, would that increase or decrease the volume of water? What about the height of the water?

Write your answer here.

Draw / Color

Loch Ness

🦕 Did you know Scotland's Loch Ness is so deep it holds **more water than all the lakes in England and Wales combined** — perfect for hiding a mystery monster!!

Area and Volume

What is the volume of fresh water on the Earth?

Is the volume of the Pacific Ocean included in this? Why or why not?

Write your answer here.

Draw / Color

Pacific Ocean

*Did you know the Pacific Ocean is so huge it covers **more area than all the land on Earth combined** — over **60 million square miles** of water!*

Area and Volume

Step # 1

What is the approximate volume of water in the Pacific Ocean?

Write your answer here.

Draw / Color

Surfing

🏄 *Did you know the biggest surfed wave ever was over **100 feet tall** — taller than a 10-story building!*

Area and Volume

What is the total estimated volume of the oceans on Earth?

Think about how many oceans there are. Are they all as big as the Pacific?

Write your answer here.

Draw / Color

Moon

Did you know the Moon always shows us the same face — because it spins once on its axis every time it orbits Earth?

Area and Volume

Step # 1

What is the volume of the Earth's only moon, the Moon?

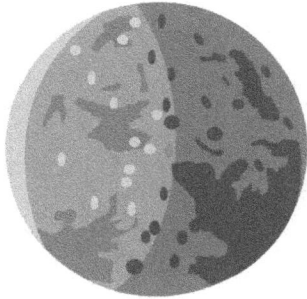

Does this include any water volume?

Write your answer here.

Draw / Color

Moons

Did you know Earth has one moon, but Jupiter has **95** — enough for a whole neighborhood of moons!

Area and Volume
Activity 149

What is the volume of the Earth?

Think about the types of matter that make up the Earth's volume.   What type is at the center of the Earth?

Draw / Color

Fresh Water

💧 *Did you know only about **3% of all water on Earth** is fresh — and most of that is frozen in glaciers and ice caps?*

Population Density

Activity 150

Step # 1

How many people does your school bus seat?

How many people could the bus hold if we used ALL the space?

Write your answer here.

Draw / Color

School Bus

🚌 *Did you know a full-size school bus is about **40 feet long** and can carry on average **70 kids** — that's like a rolling classroom!*

Population Density

Activity 151

How many students fit in a 5 ft x 5 ft area?

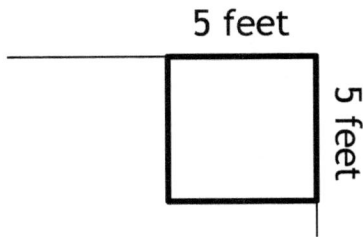

5 feet

5 feet

Choose a corner of your room. Mark a point 5 feet from the corner of one wall. Mark a point 5 feet from the other wall. Make lines from the corner to those points to create a 25 square foot area.

Write your answer here.

Draw / Color

Population Density

👥 *Did you know New York City has about **27,000 people per square mile**, while Alaska has only **1 person per square mile**?*

Population Density

Activity 152

Step # 1

How many students would fit in your classroom?

How many of those 25 ft² areas will fit in your classroom? Measure the length and width of your room, then estimate the number of students your class will hold.

Write your answer here.

Draw / Color

Overpopulation

🌑 *Did you know the world's population just passed **8 billion people** — and it's still growing every day? live there?*

Population Density

Activity 153

How many students would fit in the common area of your school?
Cafeteria? Library? Gymnasium?

How many students are there in reality for each area?

Write your answer here.

Draw / Color

Gymnasium

🏀 *Did you know a high school gym can hold more than **1,000 people** — and cover the same area as **three basketball courts** side by side?*

Population Density

Activity 154

Step # 1

What is your town or city's population density?

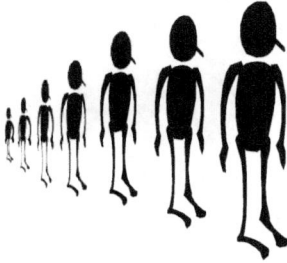

In other words, what is the average number of citizens per square foot in your locality ?

Write your answer here.

Draw / Color

Town vs. City

🏠 *Did you know the main difference between a town and a city isn't size alone — it's how they're governed and how many people live there?*

Density

Activity 155

What is the density of water at room temperature?

Draw / Color

Would the density of water change much if it were heated to twice that temperature?

Density

Activity 156

Step # 1

What is the average density of a human body?

Write your answer here.

Draw / Color

Think about what primary substance composes the body.

Density

What is the density of a vacuum
generated by a mechanical pump?

Write your answer here.

🧠 What Is Density?
Density tells us **how tightly something's packed together**.
It compares how *heavy* something is to how *big* it is.
So two things can be the same size but have **different weights**
— like a rock and a sponge!

⚖️ The Math
The formula is:
Density = Mass ÷ Volume
👉 **Mass** means how much matter is in something (we
measure it with a scale — in grams).
👉 **Volume** means how much space it takes up (we measure
it in cubic centimeters, milliliters, or liters).

Density

Activity 158

Step # 1

What is the mean density of the planet Saturn?

Remember that Saturn is one of the great Gas Giants. Do you think that would make it more or less dense than the Earth?

Write your answer here.

🗨 What Is Density?

Density tells us **how tightly something's packed together**.
It compares how *heavy* something is to how *big* it is.
So two things can be the same size but have **different weights** — like a rock and a sponge!

⚖ The Math

The formula is:

Density = Mass ÷ Volume

👉 **Mass** means how much matter is in something (we measure it with a scale — in grams).

👉 **Volume** means how much space it takes up (we measure it in cubic centimeters, milliliters, or liters).

Density

Activity 159

What is the average density of a human body AFTER INHALING?

What was the average density of the human body? What would air do to that density?

Write your answer here.

🧠 **What Is Density?**

Density tells us **how tightly something's packed together**.
It compares how *heavy* something is to how *big* it is.
So two things can be the same size but have **different weights** — like a rock and a sponge!

⚖️ **The Math**

The formula is:

Density = Mass ÷ Volume

👉 **Mass** means how much matter is in something (we measure it with a scale — in grams).

👉 **Volume** means how much space it takes up (we measure it in cubic centimeters, milliliters, or liters).

Density

Activity 160

Step # 1

If 1 gram of aluminum has the same volume as about 7.3 grams of gold. Which is denser?

Aluminum has a density of 0.098 pounds/ cubic inch (2.702 g / cm³).

Write your answer here.

❄ Example

If you have a **wood block** that weighs **200 grams** and takes up **100 cubic centimeters** of space:

Density = 200 ÷ 100 = 2 grams per cubic centimeter (g/cm^3)

That means every "cube" of wood (1 cm^3) weighs 2 grams.

💧 Compare It!

Water has a density of **1 g/cm^3**

If something's *less dense* than water (like oil or wood), it **floats**

If it's *more dense* (like a rock or metal), it **sinks**

Density

Activity 161

What is the average density of iron?

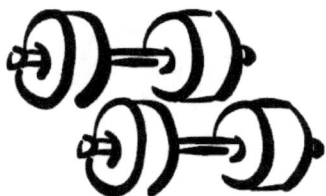

You can calculate the density by measuring the weight and volume of a block of iron. How could you measure the volume of an irregular shape of iron?

Write your answer here.

🗨 What Is Density?

Density tells us **how tightly something's packed together**.

It compares how *heavy* something is to how *big* it is.

So two things can be the same size but have **different weights** — like a rock and a sponge!

⚖ The Math

The formula is:

Density = Mass ÷ Volume

👉 **Mass** means how much matter is in something (we measure it with a scale — in grams).

👉 **Volume** means how much space it takes up (we measure it in cubic centimeters, milliliters, or liters).

Density

Activity 162

Step # 1

What is the density of mercury (the element?)

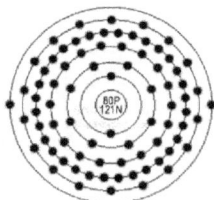

Is it more or less dense than water?

Write your answer here.

🧠 What Is Density?

Density tells us **how tightly something's packed together**.
It compares how *heavy* something is to how *big* it is.
So two things can be the same size but have **different weights** — like a rock and a sponge!

⚖️ The Math

The formula is:
Density = Mass ÷ Volume

👉 **Mass** means how much matter is in something (we measure it with a scale — in grams).

👉 **Volume** means how much space it takes up (we measure it in cubic centimeters, milliliters, or liters).

Density
Activity 163

What is the approximate density of the nucleus of an atom?

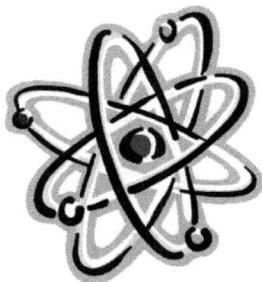

Think about anything that could be denser than that!

Write your answer here.

🧠 What Is Density?
Density tells us **how tightly something's packed together**.
It compares how *heavy* something is to how *big* it is.
So two things can be the same size but have **different weights** — like a rock and a sponge!

⚖️ The Math
The formula is:
Density = Mass ÷ Volume
👉 **Mass** means how much matter is in something (we measure it with a scale — in grams).
👉 **Volume** means how much space it takes up (we measure it in cubic centimeters, milliliters, or liters).

Density

Activity 164

Step # 1

Lithium is an ingredient in batteries. What is the weight of a lithium cube that is 12 inches on each side?

Think about the density of lithium. If you don't remember exactly, what order of magnitude is it?

How would you handle the real battery differently?

Write your answer here.

🗨 What Is Density?

Density tells us **how tightly something's packed together**.
It compares how *heavy* something is to how *big* it is.
So two things can be the same size but have **different weights** — like a rock and a sponge!

⚖ The Math

The formula is:
Density = Mass ÷ Volume

👉 **Mass** means how much matter is in something (we measure it with a scale — in grams).

👉 **Volume** means how much space it takes up (we measure it in cubic centimeters, milliliters, or liters).

Power and Energy

What is the maximum horsepower an Olympic Athlete can expend in 30 seconds?

What is meant by the term horsepower?

Write your answer here.

⚡ What Is Energy?

Energy is what makes things happen.

It's the **ability to do work** — to move, light up, heat up, or make sound.

Everything that moves or changes uses energy!

🏃 When you run, you use energy.

💡 When a light turns on, electrical energy changes to light and heat.

🍎 When you eat food, your body turns it into energy to move and grow.

Power and Energy

Step # 1

How much power is produced by a typical fireplace?

- The watt is the SI unit for power.
- The watt is equal to one Joule per second.
- The Joule is the SI unit of energy or   work

Write your answer here.

⚙ What Is Power?

Power tells us **how fast energy is used or made.**

It's like how quickly you can spend your energy!

🕐 **Power = Energy ÷ Time**

That means:

- If you use **the same energy** but do it **faster**, you have **more power**.

- If you take longer, you have **less power.**

Power and Energy

How much power is generated by a powerful car engine?

How might the driver effect the output of power from a car?

Write your answer here.

⚡ What Is Energy?

Energy is what makes things happen.

It's the **ability to do work** — to move, light up, heat up, or make sound.

Everything that moves or changes uses energy!

🏃 When you run, you use energy.

💡 When a light turns on, electrical energy changes to light and heat.

🍎 When you eat food, your body turns it into energy to move and grow.

Power and Energy
Activity 168

Step # 1

How much power does the African country of Togo generate?

Write your answer here.

⚙️ **What Is Power?**

Power tells us **how fast energy is used or made.**

It's like how quickly you can spend your energy!

🕐 **Power = Energy ÷ Time**

That means:

• If you use **the same energy** but do it **faster**, you have **more power**.

• If you take longer, you have **less power.**

Power and Energy

How much power is produced by a typical nuclear reactor?

Write your answer here.

⚡ What Is Energy?

Energy is what makes things happen.

It's the **ability to do work** — to move, light up, heat up, or make sound.

Everything that moves or changes uses energy!

🏃 When you run, you use energy.

💡 When a light turns on, electrical energy changes to light and heat.

🍎 When you eat food, your body turns it into energy to move and grow.

Power and Energy
Activity 170

Step # 1
What is the mass-energy of a single proton?

<u>Mass-energy?</u> The physical principle that measured quantities of mass and energy are equivalent can be called 'mass-energy equivalence'.
Einstein's famous equation expresses this idea:
$$E = mc^2$$
E is energy, m is mass, c is speed of light

Write your answer here.

⚙ What Is Power?
Power tells us **how fast energy is used or made.**
It's like how quickly you can spend your energy!
🕐 **Power = Energy ÷ Time**
That means:
- If you use **the same energy** but do it **faster**, you have **more power**.
- If you take longer, you have **less power.**

Power and Energy
Activity 171

How much energy is in a piece of apple pie?

How far would you need to run in order to burn up these calories?

Write your answer here.

⚡ What Is Energy?

Energy is what makes things happen.

It's the **ability to do work** — to move, light up, heat up, or make sound.

Everything that moves or changes uses energy!

🏃 When you run, you use energy.

💡 When a light turns on, electrical energy changes to light and heat.

🍎 When you eat food, your body turns it into energy to move and grow.

Power and Energy
Activity 172

Step # 1
How much energy is produced by a burning match?

Write your answer here.

⚙ What Is Power?
Power tells us **how fast energy is used or made.**

It's like how quickly you can spend your energy!

🕐 **Power = Energy ÷ Time**

That means:

•If you use **the same energy** but do it **faster**, you have **more power**.

•If you take longer, you have **less power.**

Power and Energy
Activity 173

How much energy is in a whole apple pie?

How long would you need to run to burn up these calories?

Write your answer here.

⚡ What Is Energy?

Energy is what makes things happen.

It's the **ability to do work** — to move, light up, heat up, or make sound.

Everything that moves or changes uses energy!

🏃 When you run, you use energy.

💡 When a light turns on, electrical energy changes to light and heat.

🍎 When you eat food, your body turns it into energy to move and grow.

Power and Energy
Activity 174

Step # 1

How much energy is required to vaporize a pound of water (change it from liquid to steam)?

What does 'BTU' stand for?

Write your answer here.

⚙ What Is Power?

Power tells us **how fast energy is used or made.**

It's like how quickly you can spend your energy!

🕐 **Power = Energy ÷ Time**

That means:

•If you use **the same energy** but do it **faster**, you have **more power.**

•If you take longer, you have **less power.**

Power, Energy and Other Topics

Activity 175

How much energy in kilowatt-hours does an average American household use in one year?

Check your electric bills to see how many you use in a month. How and why might it differ from month to month?

Write your answer here.

⚡ What Is Energy?

Energy is what makes things happen.

It's the **ability to do work** — to move, light up, heat up, or make sound.

Everything that moves or changes uses energy!

🏃 When you run, you use energy.

💡 When a light turns on, electrical energy changes to light and heat.

🍎 When you eat food, your body turns it into energy to move and grow.

Power and Energy
Activity 176

Step # 1

How much energy does it take to heat an average house for one year?

What are some sources of energy that people use to heat their homes?

Write your answer here.

⚙ What Is Power?

Power tells us **how fast energy is used or made.**

It's like how quickly you can spend your energy!

🕐 **Power = Energy ÷ Time**

That means:

• If you use **the same energy** but do it **faster**, you have **more power**.

• If you take longer, you have **less power.**

Power and Energy

Activity 177

How much energy was released in the
2004 Indian Ocean earthquake?

Write your answer here.

⚡ **What Is Energy?**

Energy is what makes things happen.

It's the **ability to do work** — to move, light up, heat up, or make sound.

Everything that moves or changes uses energy!

🏃 When you run, you use energy.

💡 When a light turns on, electrical energy changes to light and heat.

🍎 When you eat food, your body turns it into energy to move and grow.

Power and Energy

Step # 1
What is the theoretical total mass-energy of the Earth?

Remember that mass-energy equivalence is the principle that an amount of mass is equivalent to an amount of energy. This is described by:

$$E = mc^2$$

Write your answer here.

⚙ What Is Power?
Power tells us **how fast energy is used or made.**
It's like how quickly you can spend your energy!
🕑 **Power = Energy ÷ Time**
That means:
•If you use **the same energy** but do it **faster**, you have **more power.**
•If you take longer, you have **less power.**

Power and Energy

What is the voltage of a AA battery?

What is voltage?

Write your answer here.

⚡ What Is Energy?

Energy is what makes things happen.

It's the **ability to do work** — to move, light up, heat up, or make sound.

Everything that moves or changes uses energy!

🏃 When you run, you use energy.

💡 When a light turns on, electrical energy changes to light and heat.

🍎 When you eat food, your body turns it into energy to move and grow.

Power and Energy
Activity 180

Step # 1

How much does a kilowatt hour cost in your local area?

What is a kilowatt hour (kW-h)? How much can you do with a kW-h of energy?

Write your answer here.

⚙ What Is Power?

Power tells us **how fast energy is used or made.**

It's like how quickly you can spend your energy!

🕐 **Power = Energy ÷ Time**

That means:

•If you use **the same energy** but do it **faster**, you have **more power**.

•If you take longer, you have **less power.**

Pressure

What is the Earth's standard atmospheric pressure at sea level?

What happens to that pressure at higher altitudes?

Write your answer here.

🗨 What Is Pressure?

Pressure is how **hard** something pushes on a surface.

It tells us **how much force** is spread over **how much area**.

Think of it like this:

• If you stand on one foot, all your weight pushes on a small spot — **high pressure!**

• If you stand on two feet, the same weight spreads out — **lower pressure!**

🧮 The Math Behind Pressure

Pressure = Force ÷ Area

👉 **Force** is how hard something pushes (measured in *newtons*).

👉 **Area** is the space that force covers (measured in *square centimeters* or *square meters*).

Pressure

Step # 1

How much pressure is in a typical road bike tire?

Why does higher pressure help the riders go faster? Do mountain bikers need the same advantages?

Write your answer here.

What Is Pressure?

Pressure is how **hard** something pushes on a surface.

It tells us **how much force** is spread over **how much area**.

Think of it like this:

•If you stand on one foot, all your weight pushes on a small spot — **high pressure!**

•If you stand on two feet, the same weight spreads out — **lower pressure!**

The Math Behind Pressure

Pressure = Force ÷ Area

👉 **Force** is how hard something pushes (measured in *newtons*).

👉 **Area** is the space that force covers (measured in *square centimeters* or *square meters*).

Pressure

What is the pressure at the deepest parts of the ocean?

The deepest part of the ocean is over 35,000 feet deep (6.6 miles).

Write your answer here.

🐚 What Is Pressure?

Pressure is how **hard** something pushes on a surface.
It tells us **how much force** is spread over **how much area**.
Think of it like this:

• If you stand on one foot, all your weight pushes on a small spot — **high pressure!**

• If you stand on two feet, the same weight spreads out — **lower pressure!**

🧮 The Math Behind Pressure

Pressure = Force ÷ Area

👉 **Force** is how hard something pushes (measured in *newtons*).

👉 **Area** is the space that force covers (measured in *square centimeters* or *square meters*).

Cost

Step # 1
What is the largest bill printed in the US?

Is there really a
one-million-dollar bill?

Write your answer here.

💵 Is There a Million-Dollar Bill?
Did you know the U.S. has never made a real million-dollar bill for people to spend? The biggest U.S. bill ever printed was the **$100,000 bill.** It showed President **Woodrow Wilson** and was used **only by banks**, not by people shopping in stores.

Today, the **largest bill in circulation** is the **$100 bill** — the one with **Benjamin Franklin's** face on it!

🧮 Math Connection:
If you had a **real million dollars** all in **$100 bills**, your stack would be over **3½ feet tall** — about the height of a 4th grader's desk!

If you stacked **10,000 $100 bills**, you'd have **one million dollars** — and your money tower would be about **43 inches tall!**

Compact Scaleville Daily Reference:
Length/Distance Activities 1-34

Activity Number	Object	Powers of Ten	Best Standard Measure		Best Metric Measure		x10	x 1/10
1	1 mile from School	0 and 1	1	mile	1.6	km	charity run, typical	a city block, or the shortest possible AM radio band wavelength (1600 kHz)
2	giraffe's neck	0 and 1	6 ft		1.8	m	male sperm whale, avg.	desk-top stapler
3	your height	1 and 2	67 in		1.7	m	semi trailer	graphing calculator, or small owl
4	student desk height	1 and 2	30 in		76	cm	big "small boat", or good snow skiing base	action figures
5	flea jump	1 and 2	13 in		33	cm	deluxe patio umbrella, height	match book, width
6	paperback book length	0 and 1	7.5 in		19	cm	full bed, length	clear tape OR thin cayenne pepper, width
7	smallest bird	0 and 1	2.5 in		6.4	cm	mid-sized TV, along diagonal	red ant, large
8	granulated sugar	-2 and -1	3.94E-02 in		1	mm	paper clip, width	skeletal muscle cell
9	human red blood cell	-4 and -3	3.14E-04 in		8	micron	human hair, avg. width	dust particle, small
10	HIV Virus	-6 and -5	3.54E-06 in		90	nm	small bacterium	X-rays, longest
11	width of DNA helix	-8 and -7	7.87E-08 in		2	nm	bacterial flagellum, thickness	cesium atom, radius
12	width of gecko toe hair	-6 and -5	7.87E-06 in		200	nm	two small bacterium	nanotechnology inventions (sensors, memory cells)
13	length of E. coli genome	-2 and -1	3.94E-02 in		1	mm	game-board checker, thickness	cell body of a motor neuron
14	spring rose beetle larvae	0 and 1	1 in		2.54	cm	tarantulas' leg span	strawberry weevil
15	your hand length	0 and 1	6.9 in		17.5	cm	large mountain goat, length	fisher spider, large
16	nickel ($0.05) circumference	0 and 1	2.47 in		6.28	cm	necklace length, typical	bed bug, length
17	CD-ROM diameter	0 and 1	4.68 in		11.9	cm	elk stride, long	mosquito, large
18	neck circumference	1 and 2	12 in		31	cm	male tiger, large	sniper bullet
19	arm span	0 and 1	5 ft		1.524	m	oak tree	6" sub sandwich
20	eagle's wingspan	0 and 1	6 ft		1.8	m	from baseball pitcher's mound to home plate	one of the world's smallest dogs (Chihuahua)

Compact Scaleville Daily Reference:
Length/Distance Activities 1-34

Activity Number	Object	Powers of Ten	Best Standard Measure	Best Metric Measure	x10	x 1/10
20	eagle's wingspan	0 and 1	6 ft	1.8 m	from baseball pitcher's mound to home plate	one of the world's smallest dogs (Chihuahua)
21	chalkboard	0 and 1	8 ft	2.438 m	tall tree, pecan or sycamore	mini bonsai tree
22	giraffe's height	1 and 2	19 ft	5.8 m	leaning Tower of Pisa	Standard Schnauzer height
23	oak tree	1 and 2	50 ft	15.24 m	Pyramid of Giza	panda bear, height
24	Statue of Liberty	2 and 3	153 ft	46.5 m	tallest skyscrapers, Petronas Twin Towers in Malaysia	sports bleacher, length
26	Eiffel Tower	3 and 4	1050 ft	320 m	water-depth drilling record	original Erie Canal locks, or Diplodacus, large dinosaur
25	Pentagon wall	2 and 3	921 ft	281 m	mean ocean depth	Boeing 737-200
27	1.5 miles from School	0 and 1	1.5 miles	2.41 km	Nantucket, length	thread on a sewing spool
28	Mt. Everest	0 and 1	5.49 miles	8850 m	The Panama Canal	two Empire State Buildings
29	Grand Canyon's length	2 and 3	277 miles	446 km	Atlanta, GA to San Francisco, CA	Napa Valley
30	3000 miles from town	3 and 3	3000 miles	4,828 km	Jupiter's 'Red Spot' at its longest	longest glacier
31	Earth's equatorial radius	3 and 4	3963.189 miles	6378.135 km	mid-ocean ridge	Many NASCAR races
32	Nile River length	3 and 4	4130 miles	6647 km	mid-ocean ridge	GA-FLA state line to Miami, FLA
33	geostationary orbit altitude	4 and 5	2.22E+04 miles	3.58E+04 km	distance from Earth to Moon	The Appalachian Trail
34	tern (bird) migration	4 and 5	2.20E+04 miles	3.54E+04 km	distance from Earth to Moon	Atlantic Coastal Plain

Compact Scaleville Daily Reference:
Length/Distance Activities 35-37

Activity Number	Object	Powers of Ten	Best Standard Measure	Best Metric Measure	x10	x 1/10
35	distance from Earth to Moon	5 and 6	2.39E+05 miles	3.84E+05 km	Neptune to Nereid (Neptune's moon)	geostationary orbit, altitude
36	distance from Earth to Sun	7 and 8	9.32E+07 miles	1.50E+08 km	Pluto to Quaoar (a planetoid)	165 Walt Disney World buses annually, distance traveled
37	Milky Way diameter	5 and 6	100,000 light years	30.6 kilo-parsec	galaxy to galaxy	Earth to Cassiopeia A
37	Milky Way diameter	17 and 18	5.87E+17 miles	9.45E+17 km	galaxy to galaxy	Earth to Cassiopeia A

Speed Activities 38-58

Activity Number	Object	Powers of Ten	Best Standard Measure	Best Metric Measure	x10	x 1/10
38	Legal Highway Speed	1 and 2	65 mph	105 kph	B-52 flight, OR Mt. St. Helens eruption	industrial hydraulic drilling
39	You running	0 and 1	6.7 mph	10.7 kph	avg. rain-Asheville, NC & Columbus, OH	snowfall in Montgomery, Alabama
40	Spider's Speed	0 and 1	1.17 mph	1.89 kph	continental drift off S. America	sea level rise, 1946 and 1956
41	record breaking snail	-2 and -1	0.092 in / sec	0.23 cm / sec	three-toed sloth	tape on a heart-rate monitor
42	average hair growth	0 and 1	3.72 in / year	9.46 cm / year	Top legal highway speed	slow scuba ascent for deep dives
43	continental drift under N. America	0 and 1	2.2 in / year	4 cm / year	very fast runner	Half the Speed of a Tortoise
44	moles surface digging	0 and 1	0.2 in / sec	5.1 mm / sec	welding speed	iceberg drift
45	giant tortoise	0 and 1	3 in / sec	7.6 cm / sec	hike uphill in rocky terrain	spider
46	baby crawling	1 and 2	12 in / sec	0 m / sec	Gulf Stream flow, avg.	adult wood turtle
47	fast walker	0 and 1	4 mph	6 kph	catamaran sailing record	casual walker
48	bumble bee flying	1 and 2	11 mph	18 kph	spine tailed swift	scuba diver with a scooter
49	butterfly flying	1 and 2	20 mph	32 kph	Nascar racing car	Mississippi River in St. Louis
50	fast runner	1 and 2	27 mph	43.4 kph	Formula 1 race cars	average hike, normal walk
51	speed skater	1 and 2	27 mph	43.5 kph	falling bullet, fired into the air	push-lawn mower, max
52	Wright plane flight	1 and 2	30 mph	48.3 kph	Comet 1 plane	electric scooter
53	fastest giraffe	1 and 2	32 mph	51.5 kph	commercial jet flight	Olympic Swimmer
54	fast windsurfer	1 and 2	48 mph	77.2 kph	speed of sound in air	trotting horse
55	racing cycle	1 and 2	49 mph	79 kph	Earth's rotational speed	Bell helicopter record
56	attack submarine	1 and 2	55 mph	89 kph	Volcanic explosion on Io (Jupiter's moon)	"Incredible Tornado" wind speeds
57	cheetah	1 and 2	70 mph	112.6 kph	fastest winds in solar system (Uranus' moon)	top speed of F4F Grumman Wildcat, WWII fighter plane
58	hockey slap shot	2 and 3	110 mph	177 kph	Chuck Yeager's 1953 speed record	domestic pig

Compact Scaleville Daily Reference:
Speed Activities 59-69

Activity Number	Object	Powers of Ten	Best Standard Measure	Best Metric Measure	x10	x 1 / 10
59	terminal velocity of skydiver	2 and 3	124 mph	200 kph	space shuttle at booster separation	squirrel
60	downhill ski record	2 and 3	129 mph	207.6 kph	Apollo-10 lunar orbit	fast sailboat
61	top standard car speed	2 and 3	163 mph	262 kph	Mars Global Surveyor in orbit	average cycling speed
62	nerve impulse	2 and 3	268 mph	120 m / sec	Stardust Space Probe	charging elephant
63	Bell helicopter speed	2 and 3	315 mph	507 kph	solar waves from solar quake	max tropical depression wind
64	speed of sound in air	2 and 3	761 mph	1,225 kph	gas exhaust from planetary nebula	Six Flag's X roller coaster
65	speed of sound in concrete	3 and 4	6,934 mph	11,160 kph	escape velocity from the Sun	max speed to eject from a plane
66	Apollo 10 return	4 and 5	24,791 mph	39,897 kph	theoretical physics/ science fiction	atoms at room temp
67	Earth's orbital velocity	4 and 5	66,661 mph	107,280 kph	powered wheelchairs, max	Record air speed
68	Helios B satellite	5 and 6	1.49E+05 mph	2.40E+05 kph	basalt lava flow	Escape velocity from Mars
69	speed of light	8 and 9	9.84E+08 ft / sec	3.00E+08 m / sec	three-toed sloth	electron in cathode ray tube

Mass and Weight Activities 70-87

Activity Number	Object	Powers of Ten	Best Standard Measure	Best Metric Measure	x10	x 1 / 10
70	electron	-28 and 27	metric g	9.11E-28 g	muon	neutrino, largest possible
71	proton	-24 and -23	metric g	1.67E-24 g	lithium atom	muon
72	water molecule	-23 and -22	metric g	3.0E-23 g	caffeine molecule	hydrogen molecule (2 hydrogen atoms)
73	average human cell	-12 and -11	2.2E-12 lb	1.0E-09 g	ideal fingerprint required to extract DNA	minimum fingerprint required to extract DNA
74	lethal dose of ricin	-6 and -5	7E-06 ounce	200 micrograms	grain of sand, medium	grain of sand, small
75	mosquito	-3 and -2	1.76E-03 ounce	5.0E-02 g	radio transmitter for a cricket	two rain drops
76	golf ball	0 and 1	1.6 ounce	45 g	big box of cereal	a nickel ($0.05)
77	baby rabbit	0 and 1	1 lb	0.45 kg	big bag of potatoes	1 golf ball
78	10-week-old kitten	1 and 2	24.5 ounce	0.7 kg	large bald eagle	small chocolate bar
79	blades, pads, helmet	1 and 1	10 lb	4.5 kg	avg. 6th grader	baby rabbit
80	racing cycle	1 and 2	18 lb	8.2 kg	adult male human	dozen jumbo eggs
81	big dog	1 and 2	70 lb	31.7 kg	paper 1 person uses in 1 year	newborn human
82	human adult male	2 and 3	175.5 lb	79.6 kg	a large elk	Tasmanian devil, large
83	dolphin	2 and 3	240 lb	109 kg	Cessna plane	watermelon, large but typical
84	adult male alligator	2 and 3	500 lb	223 kg	heaviest rhinoceros	airline carry-on, max allowed
85	baby grand piano	2 and 3	700 lb	317.5 kg	parking lift	airline checked baggage, max
86	largest marsupial (extinct)	3 and 4	6,173 lb	2,800 kg	strawberries consumed at a Wimbledon tournament	big sumo wrestler
87	racehorse	3 and 3	1,000 lb	454.00 kg	street sweeper truck	petite adult female human

Compact Scaleville Daily Reference:
Mass and Weight Activities 88-105

Activity Number	Object	Powers of Ten	Best Standard Measure		Best Metric Measure		x10	x 1 / 10
88	small car	3 and 4	2,000	lb	907.00	kg	max load for a 56 ft tall crane	tuna fish, large
89	male African Elephant	0 and 1	7.5 to	ns	6.8	k g	locomotives	Formula 1 race car
90	loaded 18-wheeler	1 and 2	40	tons	36.3	metric tons	crabs eaten every day in Shanghai, China (2003)	large palette truck
91	loaded rail car	1 and 2	56	tons	50.8	metric tons	Navy's Sea Shadow experimental craft (IX 529)	adult elephant, mid-sized
92	avg. 3 bedroom house	2 and 3	125	tons	113	metric tons	light load on a standard barge	Hubble Telescope
93	707 Jet Airliner	2 and 3	175	tons	158.75	metric tons	oil rig tug boat, full	copper boulder in Lake Superior
94	International Space Station	2 and 3	206	tons	187	metric tons	Space Shuttle at launch	bell of London's Big Ben
95	ladle of molten steel, large	2 and 3	500	tons	450	metric tons	bridge tower, large	sperm whale
96	attack class sub	4 and 5	3.00E+04	tons	2.72E+04	metric tons	crude oil tanker	jumbo river barge
97	Pyramid of Giza	6 and 7	7E+06	tons	6E+06	metric tons	steel recycled from cars (2000)	largest loaded ship
98	concrete in world's largest dam	7 and 8	7E+07	tons	6E+07	metric tons	cement produced in China (2002)	Pyramid of Giza
99	world population of krill	8 and 9	6.0E+08	tons	5.4E+08	metric tons	CO_2 released annually from U.S.	concrete in world's largest dam
100	Earth's atmosphere	19 and 20	metric	kg	5.1E+15	metric tons	salt in the oceans & seas	Elara, Jupiter small moon
101	Earth's oceans	18 and 19	2.98E+21	lb	1.35E+18	metric tons	Pluto	Enceladus, Saturn moon
102	the Earth	21 and 22	metric	kg	5.9E+21	metric tons	Uranus	Mars
103	Jupiter	24 and 25	metric	kg	1.9E+24	metric tons	Neptune	brown dwarf star, small
104	Sun	30 and 31	metric	kg	2.0E+27	metric tons	small supergiant star	minimum to burn hydrogen through fusion
105	Milky Way Galaxy	42 and 43	metric	kg	2.0E+39	metric tons	Universe (observable)	Sagittarius A, a black hole

Area and Volume Activities 106-112

Activity Number	Object	Powers of Ten	Best Standard Measure		Best Metric Measure		x10	x 1 / 10
106	computer pixel	-5 and -4	8.53E-05	in²	0.055	mm²	RFID chip	average cross-section of 'fast-twitch' fibers in a sprinter
107	flat-head pin	-3 and 2	3E-03	in²	2	mm²	a computer smart card microcontroller	opening in a dental cleaner, where the gas flows through
108	postage stamp	0 and 1	0.775	in²	5	cm²	bridge playing cards	small mineral particle
109	airline food tray	0 and 1	1.08	ft²	1,000	cm²	surfboard	candy bar wrapper
110	6 sq.ft. plot of land	0 and 1	6.00	ft²	1	m²	office for 2 mid-level employees	Min cage space for laying hens in the European Union
111	skin area	1 and 2	20	ft²	2	m²	double dormitory room	cloth in a small dog sweater
112	ping-pong table	1 and 2	45	ft²	4	m²	efficiency apartment	30" LCD TV

Compact Scaleville Daily Reference:
Area Activities 113-125

Activity Number	Object	Powers of Ten	Best Standard Measure		Best Metric Measure		x10	x 1 / 10
113	parking space	1 and 2	12	yd^2	10	m^2	1/2 a tennis court	largest standard paper, International A0
114	classroom ceiling	2 and 2	100	yd^2	84	m^2	urban lot-size	private veggie garden
115	American football field	3 and 4	6,396	yd^2	5,348	m^2	large exhibition hall	median house lot in Arizona
116	Great Pyramid of Giza, base	1 and 2	13.6	acres	55,000	m^2	Vatican City	American Football Field
117	Pentagon building	1 and 2	29	acres	0.12	km^2	Secret Garden inside Beijing's Imperial Palace	Royal Park, largest public park in Geneva, Switzerland
118	Pentagon parking	1 and 2	67	acres	0.27	km^2	Temple of Heaven in Beijing, China	Commercial space in Las Vegas' Cosmopolitan Resort and Casino
119	Pentagon floors	2 and 3	152	acres	0.62	km^2	territory of male Giant Panda	Base of the Great Pyramid of Giza
120	Manhattan, NY	1 and 2	23.0	$mile^2$	59.5	km^2	Toronto, Canada	Average farm in South Dakota (1997)
121	Island of Bali, Indonesia	3 and 4	2200	$mile^2$	5,700	km^2	Lake Victoria, world's 2nd largest freshwater lake	Island nation of Singapore
122	Texas	5 and 6	2.673E+05	$mile^2$	6.923E+05	km^2	Australia	Lake Victoria, world's 2nd largest freshwater lake
123	US	6 and 7	3.676E+06	$mile^2$	9.520E+06	km^2	Atlantic and Arctic Oceans	New Guinea
124	Earth	8 and 9	1.97E+08	$mile^2$	5.10E+08	km^2	Sunspot Group 9169 or Neptune	surface of the Moon
125	Neptune	8 and 9	2.97E+09	$mile^2$	7.69E+09	km^2	two Saturns	two Venuses

Volume Activities 126-136

126	small sugar cube	-2 and -1	0.06	in^3	1	cm^3	2 teaspoons	tiny necklace bead
127	volume of milk carton	0 and 1	8	fl oz	237	cm^3	tea kettle	ink in an ink-jet cartridge
128	coke bottle	1 and 2	20	fl oz	0.59	liters	conservation toilet flush	pepper-spray
129	tissue box	2 and 3	147	in^3	2,410	cm^3	mid-sized microwave (800 watts)	household glass
130	party balloon	4 and 5	0.792	gal	3	liters	$491.52 in pennies, or 8 gal wet-dry vacuum, or trash bag	child's 'sippy' cup
131	cereal box	2 and 3	259	in^3	4,244	cm^3	small moving box	travel coffee mug
132	soda can radius*	1 and 2	2.5	in	6.4	cm	radius of a large starfish	cross-sectional radius of a small snail shell
133	pie tin radius*	0 and 1	4.5	in	11.43	cm	golf club swing radius	hole punch
134	pie tin diameter*	0 and 1	9	in	22.9	cm	diameter of a cupola at the Studebaker foundry	diameter of a chipotle chile
135	pie base circumference*	1 and 2	28	in	71.1	cm	circumference of large trees, Sitka Spruce, oak	circumference of a nickel
136	big tortilla circumference*	1 and 2	37.7	in	97	cm	small trampoline circumference	toilet paper holder circumference

Compact Scaleville Daily Reference:
Volume Activities 137-149

Activity Number	Object	Powers of Ten	Best Standard Measure		Best Metric Measure		x10	x 1 / 10
137	pie tin base area*	1 and 2	64	in^2	413	cm^2	backyard grilling surface	top of a flower
138	volume of pie tin	1 and 2	64	in^3	1049	cm^3	fuel tank in a 4-stroke motorcycle	uncertainty on gas pumps
139	standard large suitcase	3 and 4	6,100	in^3	1E+05	cm^3	large moving box	U.S. per capita alcohol consumption (over 21)
140	oil barrel	1 and 2	42	gal	159	liters	6-person hot-tub	commercial lawn mower gas tank
141	3-4 person hot air balloon	4 and 5	8.80E+04	ft^3	2.50E+03	m^3	solid waste generated every day in Jakarta, Indonesia	air in a 30 ft x 29 ft room with a 10 ft ceiling
142	olympic pool	5 and 6	6.60E+05	gal	2.50E+06	liters	Chevron's post-Katrina daily oil production in Gulf of Mex	landfill saved by recycling 36 tons of cardboard
143	water tower	6 and 7	3.17E+06	gal	1.2E+07	liters	Quatar's 2003 oil production	water sprayed on the Space Shuttle launch pad during a launch
144	Loch Ness	12 and 13	1.98E+12	gal	7.5	km^3	eruption from a strong Plinian volcano: like the one that formed Crater Lake	average cumulus cloud
145	fresh water on Earth	6 and 7	8.4E+06	$miles^3$	3.50E+07	km^3	Atlantic Ocean with adjacent seas	Mediterranean Sea
146	Pacific Ocean	8 and 9	1.68E+08	$miles^3$	7.00E+08	km^3	Pluto	twice the freshwater on Earth
147	Oceans on Earth	8 and 9	3.1E+08	$miles^3$	1.3E+09	km^3	Europa, Jupiter's moon	half the Indian Ocean
148	Moon	9 and 10	5.30E+09	$miles^3$	2.2E+10	km^3	Mars	Earth's total water supply
149	Earth	11 and 12	2.40E+11	$miles^3$	1.00E+12	km^3	1/6th of Neptune	two planet Mercury's

Population Density Activities 150-154

Activity Number	Object	Powers of Ten	Best Standard Measure		Best Metric Measure		x10	x 1 / 10
150	school bus passengers	1 and 2	44	people	NA	NA	Boeing 747	passenger car with baby seat
151	Students / 25 sq. ft.	1 and 2	18	people	NA	NA	Airbus A320 airplane	sports car
152	Students / classroom	2 and 3	225	people	NA	NA	mid-sized home (3000 sq ft)	small garden (30 sq. ft.)
153	Students / public areas		varies	people	NA	NA	varies	varies
154	town's population density		varies	people	NA	NA	varies	varies

Compact Scaleville Daily Reference:
Density Activities 155-164

Activity Number	Object	Powers of Ten	Best Standard Measure		Best Metric Measure		x10	x 1 / 10
155	Water	1 and 2	62.4	lb/ft³	1.00	g/cm³	lead	a snowflake
156	average human body	1 and 2	61.5	lb/ft³	0.985	g/cm³	radon, or silver	a snowflake
157	Vacuum from a mechanical pump	-5 and -4	6.2E-05	lb/ft³	1.0E-06	g/cm³	Earth's atmosphere at an altitude of 20 miles	Earth's atmosphere at an altitude of 42 miles
158	Density of Saturn	1 and 2	43.7	lb/ft³	0.7	g/cm³	Iron	powdered carbon, or lowest density of balsa wood
159	human body after inhaling	1 and 2	59.0	lb/ft³	0.950	g/cm³	nickel, the metal	medium-density insulating foams or balsa wood
160	Aluminum	2 and 3	168.7	lb/ft³	2.702	g/cm³	platinum (element)	cork (rolled oats = 19 lb/ft³)
161	Iron	2 and 3	489.9	lb/ft³	7.874	g/cm³	3.5 times the density of iridium,	course salt -or- soap
162	Mercury	2 and 3	845.7	lb/ft³	13.546	g/cm³	core of the Sun	wool
163	nucleus of an atom	16 and 17	1.25E+16	lb/ft³	2.0E+14	g/cm³	a neutron star	white dwarf star
164	Lithium	1 and 2	33.09	lbs	0.53	g/cm³	Mean Earth density	low-density industrial foams

Power Activities 165-169

Activity Number	Object	Powers of Ten	Best Standard Measure		Unit Conversion		x10	x 1 / 10
165	Olympic Athlete (max)	0 and 1	1	hp	746	W	sound system in large convention hall	household lightbulb
166	fireplace	0 and 1	1.2	kW	1.14	BTU / sec	power use per person in the U.S. (2001)	average human body output
167	a powerful car	5 and 6	200	kW	190	BTU / sec	power from a blue whale	small local radio station
168	output of the country Togo	7 and 7	10	MW	9,480	BTU / sec	770 biggest steam-electric plants in the U.S. (2005)	utility-sized wind turbine (0.7-2.5)
169	nuclear reactor	9 and 10	1.2	GW	1.1E+06	BTU / sec	world's largest hydroelectric dam	peak output of Nimitz-class aircraft carrier

Energy Activities 170-172

Activity Number	Object	Powers of Ten	Best Standard Measure		Unit Conversion		x10	x 1 / 10
170	mass-energy of proton	2 and 3	940	MeV		1.42E-13 BTU	firing neuron	energy released in fission of one plutonium or uranium atom
171	slice of apple pie	2 and 3	320	Cal	NA	NA	average Thanksgiving Day meal	one cup of broccoli
172	burning match	0 and 1	1.0	kJ	0.95	BTU	2.5 dietary Calories	energy used by a 120 watt light bulb in one sec

Compact Scaleville Daily Reference:
Energy Activities 173-178

Activity Number	Object	Powers of Ten	Best Standard Measure		Unit Conversion		x10	x 1 / 10
173	apple pie (8 slices)	3 and 4	2,560	Cal	1.07E+07	J	energy released by combustion of 1 gallon of gasoline	energy containted in a small bag of chips or candy bar
174	Vaporize 1 lb water	2 and 3	970	BTU	1.02E+06	J	light bulb left on for one day	energy released by combustion of 2 grams of gasoline
175	Average household annual consumption	4 and 4	10,000	kW-hour	3.60E+10	J	Saturn V rocket	Energy released by one ton of TNT
176	Energy to heat an average house for one year	4 and 5	2E+04	kW-hour	7.20E+10	J	Jet plane crossing the Atlantic Ocean (1-way)	Large Lightning bolt
177	2004 Indian Ocean earthquake	20 and 21	1.3E+20	J	3.69E+13	kW-hours	solar energy received in the country of Manitoba every year	total energy production in US in 2001
178	mass-energy of Earth	41 and 42	5.37E+41	J	NA	NA	supernova	released from the Sun in one year

Voltage and Energy Cost Activities 179-180

Activity Number	Object	Powers of Ten	Volts				object x 10	object / 10
179	AA battery	0 and 1	1.5	V			first Christmas lights	lemmon battery'
180	cost of kilowatt-hour	0 and 1						

Pressure Bonus Activities B1-B3

Activity Number	Object	Powers of Ten (PSI)	Best Standard Measure		Unit Conversion		x10	x 1 / 10
B-1	atmospheric pressure	1 and 2	1	atmosphere	1.01E+05	Pascal (Pa)	small steam locomotive boiler	mean normal diastolic blood pressure in adult
B-2	road bike tire	1 and 2	8.3	bar	1.50E+06	Pascal (Pa)	power paint sprayer, or pressure washers	atmospheric pressure on Mars
B-3	bottom of ocean trench	3 and 4	1,000	bar	1.00E+09	Pascal (Pa)	hardness of steel	heavy duty pressure washers, or atmospheric pressure on Mars

Here are a few web sites with some good numbers:

- Go to www.onlineconversion.com for a great conversion tool.
- Grab a copy of the Factastic Book of Comparisons by Russell Ash.
- For the fun extremes, check out The Guinness Book of World Records.
- For great facts about animals and sea creatures, go to www.sandiegozoo.org and www.seaworld.org.
- The trusty online dictionary: www.m-w.com/dictionary
- Wonderful facts on European lands: www.efi.fi/fine/resources
- Fun student and educator activities are at www.enchantedlearning.com and www.grandpapencil.com.

- For information on everything, go to www.wikipedia.com.
- For helpful math tools and tips, go to www.webmath.com.
- For physics without the fear, see what's up at www.fearofphysics.com.
- To learn about all things astronomical, visit www.absoluteastronomy.com.
- For a primer (and pep rally) on metric units, try www.thinkmetric.org.uk.
- For population densities, the government is your source: www.census.gov/population
- Go to the US Geological Survey's Water Education site at http://ga.water.usgs.gov/edu/index.html.

www.insl.org

Art of STEM
Scaleville Series

Recognizing an unreasonable answer is difficult unless one knows how much things weigh, how fast they move, how much area they cover. Students only need a few mental landmarks to enable them to estimate to the nearest power of ten. Will the answer be closer to 20, 200, 2,000 or 20,000? As estimation skills improve, reasonableness becomes a meaningful concept.

Scaleville is a set of daily class starters. Used regularly, students will gain a sense of number. You will build fundamental skills in estimation, an understanding of measure and a physical connection to scale. How much does a racing bike weigh? How fast does it go? How fast does a baby crawl? How tall is a giraffe? How tall are you? How much, how far, how fast, how much...

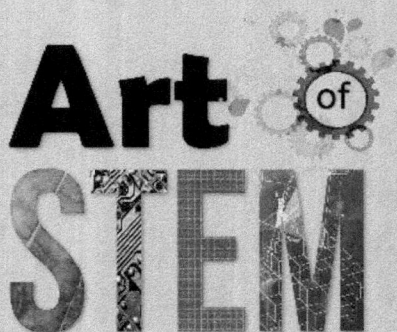

Art of
STEM